P9-CBA-695

AMERICA'S ODDEST FOODS

By Joe Yerdon

Gareth Stevens
PUBLISHING

Please visit our website, www.garethstevens.com. For a free color catalog of all our high-quality books, call toll free 1-800-542-2595 or fax 1-877-542-2596.

Library of Congress Cataloging-in-Publication Data

Yerdon, Joe, author.
 America's oddest foods / Joe Yerdon.
     pages cm — (Weird America)
 Includes index.
 ISBN 978-1-4824-4012-6 (pbk.)
 ISBN 978-1-4824-4011-9 (6 pack)
 ISBN 978-1-4824-4013-3 (library binding)
 1. Food—United States—Miscellanea—Juvenile literature. 2. Curiosities and wonders—United States—Juvenile literature. 3. Cooking, American—Miscellanea—Juvenile literature. I. Title.
 TX360.U6Y47 2016
 641.5973—dc23

                    2015029035

First Edition

Published in 2016 by
Gareth Stevens Publishing
111 East 14th Street, Suite 349
New York, NY 10003

Copyright © 2016 Gareth Stevens Publishing

Designer: Sarah Liddell
Editor: Ryan Nagelhout

Photo credits: Cover, p. 1 (arrow) Mascha Tace/Shutterstock.com; cover, p. 1 (main) Elikapeki24/Wikimedia Commons; sidebar used throughout zayats-and-zayats/Shutterstock.com; background texture used throughout multipear/Shutterstock.com; p. 5 Joshua Resnick/Shutterstock.com; p. 6 GeeJo/Shutterstock.com; p. 7 AE.Panuwat Studio/Shutterstock.com; p. 8 (left) Andrjuss/Shutterstock.com; pp. 8 (right), 15 (inset) Glane23/Wikimedia Commons; p. 9 taurus15/Shutterstock.com; pp. 10, 11 Jonathunder/Wikimedia Commons; p. 12 Darryl Brooks/Shutterstock.com; p. 13 Fanfo/Shutterstock.com; p. 14 Solsticed/Wikimedia Commons; p. 15 (main) F Ceragioli/Wikimedia Commons; p. 16 Gregory Bull/Associated Press/AP Images; p. 17 (candy bar) Neelix/Wikimedia Commons; p. 17 (pickles) Brent Hofacker/Shutterstock.com; p. 17 (butter, Twinkie, and bacon) File Upload Bot (Magnus Manske)/Wikimedia Commons; p. 17 (mac and cheese) farbled/Shutterstock.com; p. 17 (corndog) Ekaterina Bratova/Shutterstock.com; p. 17 (Oreos) Erika J Mitchell/Shutterstock.com; p. 18 fototip/Shutterstock.com; p. 19 (top) Gaijin42/Wikimedia Commons; p. 19 (bottom) Bojangles-commonswiki/Wikimedia Commons; p. 20 Fran Rogers/Wikimedia Commons; p. 21 Douglas.flowe/Wikimedia Commons; p. 22 BorgQueen/Wikimedia Commons; p. 23 The Photographer/Wikimedia Commons; p. 24 Caliga10/Wikimedia Commons; p. 25 TheDapperDan/Wikimedia Commons; p. 26 Northamerica1000/Wikimedia Commons; p. 27 Thejinan/Wikimedia Commons; p. 28 Michael Kraus/Shutterstock.com; p. 29 Valerio Pardi/Wikimedia Commons.

Printed in the United States of America

CPSIA compliance information: Batch #CW16GS: For further information contact Gareth Stevens, New York, New York at 1-800-542-2595.

CONTENTS

Odd from Ordinary 4

Pig Parts. 6

Minnesota Mixes It Up. 10

Backyard Burgoo 12

Going West 14

Fry It Up. 16

I'm Stuffed!. 18

Eating Garbage? 20

Island Treats 22

Cincinnati Favorites 24

Time for Dessert! 26

Gelatin Fun 28

Glossary. 30

For More Information. .31

Index 32

Words in the glossary appear in **bold** type the first time they are used in the text.

ODD FROM ORDINARY

Have you ever walked into the lunchroom and smelled something odd? Have you ever had a friend tell you about a strange food he tried on a trip to another country? People may all have the same taste buds, but different people like eating all kinds of different things.

Even different parts of our country like to chow down on a variety of different foods. Your definition of "strange" may be different from other people in your school. Maybe the lunch staff is making something special from their hometown! America is full of odd meals made from even odder ingredients. Let's take a look at some of America's oddest foods!

It's How You Make It

Both "gross" and "good" foods can be found in a single animal. You might like bacon from a pig, for example, but would you eat a pig's eyeball? What about its foot? If you're a more adventurous eater, you might not find anything in this book very odd!

Some people think a dish like chicken and waffles is tasty, while others think it's gross. Would you eat them together?

5

PIG PARTS

If you like bacon, you've had pig before. Ham, bacon, and pork chops are some pig **staples**, but a lot of stranger dishes come from other parts of a pig. Feet, intestines, stomach, kidneys, and more are pig parts that are a part of some more unusual meals.

Scrapple is a popular breakfast food in eastern Pennsylvania. It's made from the heart, liver, and head of a pig. These parts are cooked down over a long time, then the fat and bones are removed. The meat is cut up finely and seasoned with cornmeal and spices. It's then made into a form that resembles meat loaf, cut into slices, and fried. Some people put maple syrup, butter, ketchup, or even jelly on their scrapple!

scrapple

chitterlings are made from pig intestines. They're a popular dish in the South, often served with collard greens, hush puppies, ham hocks, and black-eyed peas. They have to be cleaned many times before cooking to keep people from getting sick. Chitterlings are often boiled or stewed with an onion to reduce their smell!

Long ago, not using every part of an animal was viewed as wasteful since food wasn't as plentiful as it is today.

7

that doesn't make it any less strange. Pickled pigs' feet are another southern food standard. Pickled pigs' feet are made in much the same way that pickles—pickled cucumbers—are made.

The pigs' feet are salted and smoked the same way ham and bacon are treated, or cured, then "pickled" using hot vinegar brine. Brine is a salted water solution used to help keep the pigs' feet from drying out. After that, the pigs' feet are often stored in jars and put aside to eat later.

Lots of different things can be pickled, but would you eat feet kept in a jar?

Hog Maw

Hog maw is the inside lining of a pig's stomach. Hog maw can be baked, fried, stewed, or broiled. In Pennsylvania, hog maw is often stuffed with potatoes and pork sausage, then cooked with cabbage, onion, and spices. It's a New Year's Day **tradition** in some southern homes to have hog maws and chitterlings for good luck in the New Year!

9

MINNESOTA MIXES IT UP

The state of Minnesota is an odd-food paradise. Many Minnesotans have family that comes from Sweden, Finland, Norway, and Denmark. Their native foods have found their way to America, and some have added an American twist. Lutefisk may be the strangest of all these foods.

Brought over from Norway, lutefisk is made of dried whitefish soaked in cold water for 5 or 6 days, then placed in a solution of lye. Lye on its own is **corrosive** and poisonous. The fish is then put back in cold water again so it swells up.

"Jucy Lucy"

Cheeseburgers are an American staple, but Minnesota does its meat and cheese a bit differently. The "Jucy Lucy" is a burger with cheese stuffed inside the beef patty and cooked up just like a regular burger. There's an ongoing argument about which restaurant—Matt's Bar or the 5-8 Club—invented the cheesy dish.

After soaking in water for days, lutefisk is cooked and eaten. It's more like a jelly than a fish!

11

BACKYARD BURGOO

When you're in Kentucky you might think about eating fried chicken, but there's a dish you might come across that's got more of a local flavor. Burgoo is a spicy stew—like a thicker soup—made with the usual things you'd find in a stew: potatoes, carrots, onions, celery, and garlic in beef stock. What makes traditional burgoo different from beef stew is that it's often made with rabbit, venison, opossum, raccoon, or squirrel!

Modern burgoo is usually made with beef, pork, and chicken, but those animals weren't readily available back in the early 1800s when the dish was first created.

Grits

Grits may look kind of gross, but many southerners think they're delicious! They're made by boiling small, broken grains of corn in water. The corn is stirred and then seasoned with salt and pepper as well as a lot of butter. Grits go great with eggs and bacon at breakfast, but sometimes people eat them with ham or shrimp later in the day.

Early American settlers often had to eat whatever animals they could hunt nearby!

GOING WEST

When it comes to making use of every part of an animal, cows are no exception. While everyone knows you can eat cow ribs, brisket, and steak, there's another part of the animal that's used to make Rocky Mountain oysters.

Unlike oysters found in the sea, Rocky Mountain oysters are deep-fried bull testicles—their reproductive organs. To be more exact, the "oysters" are peeled and coated with flour, salt, and pepper. Sometimes they're pounded flat before they're fried! You'll find Rocky Mountain oysters mostly in Colorado, but also in Oklahoma and Texas, where they're known as "calf fries."

Frito Pie

Frito pie is a popular dish in Texas and the Southwest that has a misleading name. Frito pie isn't a dessert, but a way to eat corn chips and chili! Frito pie can be made like a casserole. People add cheese, salsa, beans, and even jalapeños on top.

Rocky Mountain oysters are also called prairie oysters or cowboy caviar!

15

FRY IT UP

It's not just foods that are deep fried, drinks get the same treatment as well. At county fairs across the country, you can find deep-fried Kool-Aid! The edible drink got its start in California. The question is: How can you fry a drink?

Here's the trick: A frying batter is made using flour, cornstarch, baking powder, and salt combined with an egg, water, and vegetable oil. When those ingredients are mixed, a thick batter is formed and Kool-Aid powder is added. With the batter and powder mixed together, scoops of the mixture are deep fried and dipped in powdered sugar.

Thanks to the magic of a deep fryer, you can eat and drink your Kool-Aid!

DEEP-FRIED EVERYTHING AT THE FAIR

candy bar

 pickles

 butter

mac and cheese

 Twinkie

corndog

 bacon

Oreos

I'M STUFFED!

When it comes to Thanksgiving, having turkey at dinner is an important part of the holiday. For some families, turkey isn't enough. They need a "turducken." A turkey is traditionally filled with stuffing made of breadcrumbs, seasoning, celery, and onions. In the case of a turducken, the turkey is instead stuffed with other meats. It's a turkey stuffed with a duck that's been stuffed with a chicken!

The chicken and duck have their bones removed to help them better fit inside each other and the turkey. The turducken became popular when a football announcer, John Madden, gave one to the winning team at a Thanksgiving football game.

The Cronut

Cronuts are **croissants** sweetened up and prepared like a doughnut. Cronuts became famous in New York City when chef Dominique Ansel fried croissants, covered them with sugar, and filled them with cream like a doughnut. While the cronut isn't very healthy to eat, its buttery sweetness has created a bakery craze! It takes up to 3 days to make one!

A "cherpumple" is a dessert inspired by the turducken. It's a three-layer cake with a cherry, apple, and pumpkin pie stuffed inside!

cherpumple

turducken

EATING GARBAGE?

Think of what it would be like to have all your favorite foods on one plate to eat. That's pretty much what you'll find in Rochester, New York, when you order a garbage plate. The first garbage plate is said to have been made at Nick Tahou Hots, where a garbage plate starts with baked beans, macaroni salad, and French fries or home fries.

Then it's topped with meat, starting with a cheeseburger, hamburger, Italian sausages, hot dogs, steak, and sometimes chicken. Eggs, fried fish, or even a grilled cheese sandwich is piled on top of this tasty—but maybe a little gross—stack of flavors.

garbage plate from Nick Tahou Hots

Sides and Napkins

Mustard, hot sauce, or onions often top off the dish, which really does all fit on one big plate. Sometimes you get a side of bread and butter. If that sounds like a lot of food and a bit of a mess, it is. That's why it's called the garbage plate!

Another restaurant in Rochester came up with a **vegan** option called a compost plate.

ISLAND TREATS

Spam is canned, precooked spiced ham that can be found just about everywhere across America. In Hawaii, however, Spam became more than just meat in a can—it's practically **mandatory** eating!

Spam became popular in Hawaii during the 1940s when it was served to the military stationed there during World War II. Since Spam was already cooked and kept in a can, it was easy to ship and didn't spoil quickly. Since then, Spam has become part of Hawaiian **culture** and found its way into many local dishes, including Spam *musubi*—fried Spam sandwiched between layers of rice and wrapped in seaweed.

Poke

Poke (POH-keh) is made from raw yellowfin tuna **marinated** in sea salt and soy sauce. It's added to roasted kukui nuts, seaweed, sesame oil, and chili pepper. The ingredients are all chopped up and served in a bowl as an **appetizer**. If tuna doesn't sound tasty, *poke* can also be made with octopus or salmon.

The state of Hawaii alone
eats more than 7 million
cans of Spam a year!

Spam musubi

CINCINNATI FAVORITES

German Americans near Cincinnati, Ohio, love to make *goetta* (GEHT-uh). *Goetta* is a ground-up meat, usually pork or both pork and beef, that's seasoned and **blended** with steel-cut or pinhead oats. The mixture is made into a loaf or sausage-like patty, then cut and fried.

Goetta was created because if you added oats to meat you could spread the protein's use over a few days. If *goetta* sounds familiar, it's often compared to scrapple. Food lovers say that, unlike scrapple, *goetta* has a bit of a "funk" to it. Who's ready to eat now?

Cincinnati Chili

Spaghetti may be one of your favorite foods, but would you pour chili on it? One Cincinnati favorite is Skyline Chili, which does just that! The chili is a secret company recipe, and cheddar cheese is piled on top of the dish. They often add onions (called a 3-Way) and beans (called a 4-Way) on top.

TIME FOR DESSERT!

Would you try something called "Eskimo ice cream"? You'd have to go to western Alaska to find *akutaq* (ah-GOO-duhk), but it's a popular dessert up there. *Akutaq* is better known as "Eskimo ice cream" and has its roots with the native peoples of Alaska and northern Canada.

The dessert is made of fresh berries found in the region, but the traditional main ingredient is whipped fat! The fat comes from fish, reindeer, caribou, walrus, polar bear, or seal oil. Modern *akutaq* is likely made with **vegetable shortening** instead of animal fat and sugar as well as berries.

Ambrosia

Ambrosia is an odd dessert made of cream, fruit, coconuts, and sometimes nuts. The cream is whipped with marshmallows to make it light and fluffy. Fruits like oranges, pineapples, cherries, and even apples or grapes are mixed in. When it's done, it sort of looks like a bowl filled with clouds!

It was **customary** for women to make akutaq after the first polar bear or seal catch of the season.

27

GELATIN FUN

Gelatins like Jell-O are popular desserts that taste like a bunch of different fruits. Making Jell-O salad with strawberries or banana is easy, but not all recipes are quite so tasty. Would you put meat, fish, or eggs in your Jell-O?

Popular cookbooks in the 1960s had a tuna and Jell-O pie recipe for families to try at home! Cottage cheese and salmon molds, sauerkraut molds, or even pressed ox tongue molds are all recipes found in old cookbooks! Many French-inspired dishes like aspic use gelatin to set meats into certain forms. Would you eat a lemony salmon tower?

What Is Gelatin, Anyway?

Gelatin is a protein made from animal parts. The skin, tendons, bones, and **ligaments** of cows or pigs are boiled in water. Gelatin is used in many things, and it's the primary ingredient in Jell-O and some puddings. It may sound gross, but it sure doesn't taste like cows or pigs!

Because gelatin can be easily molded, it was often used with meat to make meals.

29

GLOSSARY

appetizer: a food or drink served before a meal

blend: to mix together evenly

corrosive: having the power to break down matter

croissant: a flaky, moon-shaped roll

culture: the beliefs, practices, and religions of a group of people

customary: commonly done

ligament: a tough band of tissue that holds organs in place in the body or connects bones

mandatory: required

marinate: to season by soaking in a mix of liquid and spices

staple: something often in use or demand

tradition: the handing down of information, beliefs, and customs of one generation to another

vegan: a diet that does not include animal or dairy products

vegetable shortening: a fat that comes from plants and is solid at room temperature

FOR MORE INFORMATION

BOOKS

Wishinsky, Frieda, and Elizabeth MacLeod. *Everything but the Kitchen Sink: Weird Stuff You Didn't Know About Food.* New York, NY: Scholastic, 2008.

Zimmern, Andrew. *Andrew Zimmern's Field Guide to Exceptionally Weird, Wild, & Wonderful Foods: An Intrepid Eater's Digest.* New York, NY: Feiwel and Friends, 2012.

WEBSITES

Serious Eats: Recipes
seriouseats.com/recipes
Visit this site to get recipes for some of your favorite American foods.

What's Cooking America
whatscookingamerica.net/
This site is full of the stories and history of great American foods.

INDEX

akutaq 26, 27

ambrosia 26

burgoo 12

calf fries 14

cherpumple 19

chitterlings 7, 9

compost plate 21

cowboy caviar 15

cronuts 18

deep-fried bacon 17

deep-fried butter 17

deep-fried candy bar 17

deep-fried corndog 17

deep-fried Kool-Aid 16

deep-fried mac and cheese 17

deep-fried Oreos 17

deep-fried pickles 17

deep-fried Twinkie 17

"Eskimo ice cream" 26

Frito pie 14

garbage plate 20

gelatin 28, 29

goetta 24

grits 12

hog maw 9

Jell-O 28

Jucy Lucy 10

lutefisk 10, 11

Nick Tahou Hots 20

pickled pigs' feet 8

pig feet 6, 8

pig intestines 6, 7

pig stomach 6, 9

poke 22

prairie oysters 15

Rocky Mountain oysters 14, 15

scrapple 6, 24

Skyline Chili 25

Spam 22, 23

Spam musubi 22

turducken 18